Put Beginning Readers on the Right Track with
ALL ABOARD READING™

The All Aboard Reading series is especially for beginning readers. Written by noted authors and illustrated in full color, these are books that children really and truly *want* to read—books to excite their imagination, tickle their funny bone, expand their interests, and support their feelings. With four different reading levels, All Aboard Reading lets you choose which books are most appropriate for your children and their growing abilities.

Picture Readers—for Ages 3 to 6
Picture Readers have super-simple texts with many nouns appearing as rebus pictures. At the end of each book are 24 flash cards—on one side is the rebus picture; on the other side is the written-out word.

Level 1—for Preschool through First Grade Children
Level 1 books have very few lines per page, very large type, easy words, lots of repetition, and pictures with visual "cues" to help children figure out the words on the page.

Level 2—for First Grade to Third Grade Children
Level 2 books are printed in slightly smaller type than Level 1 books. The stories are more complex, but there is still lots of repetition in the text and many pictures. The sentences are quite simple and are broken up into short lines to make reading easier.

Level 3—for Second Grade through Third Grade Children
Level 3 books have considerably longer texts, use harder words and more complicated sentences.

All Aboard for happy reading!

To Bill, for all your help and support.
Special thanks to Bat Conservation International
and Paul Dyer Photography — Judith Moffatt

Thanks to Pat Thomas, Mammal Department, International Wildlife Conservation Park (Bronx Zoo).

Library of Congress Cataloging-in-Publication Data

Milton, Joyce.
    Bats : creatures of the night / by Joyce Milton ; illustrated by Judith Moffatt.
      p.   cm. — (All aboard reading.)
    Summary: Describes the physical characteristics, behavior, and habitats of different kinds of bats.
    1. Bats—Juvenile literature. [1. Bats.] I. Moffatt, Judith, ill. II. Title. III. Series.
QL737.C5M67   1993
599.4—dc20   92-43198

ISBN 0-448-40194-0 (GB) A B C D E F G H I J
ISBN 0-448-40193-2 (pbk.)   F G H I J

ALL
ABOARD
READING™

Level 2
Grades 1–3

BATS
CREATURES OF THE NIGHT

By Joyce Milton
Illustrated by Judith Moffatt

Grosset & Dunlap • New York

No one has lived

on this farm for years.

The barn looks empty.

But it isn't!

Strange creatures are sleeping

in the loft.

As the sun goes down,

they take to the air.

They come flying out
of the windows.

They swoop low over the river.

They dart under an old bridge.

From far away

the creatures look like birds.

But who ever heard

of a bird with fur?

Close up, they look like mice.

But who ever heard

of a mouse with wings?

7

These strange creatures are bats.

Bats are mammals.

Just like rabbits

and horses and dogs.

Just like us.

Many people think that bats are blind.

But that's not true.

Bats have eyes and they can see.

It's just that they spend

most of the time in the dark.

thumb

There is one thing

that makes bats different

from all other mammals.

They can fly.

Bat wings are not like bird wings.

Bats do not have feathers.

A bat's wing is really

an arm with a hand.

Its long, thin fingers

are joined by a flap of skin.

Bats even have little thumbs.

fingers

11

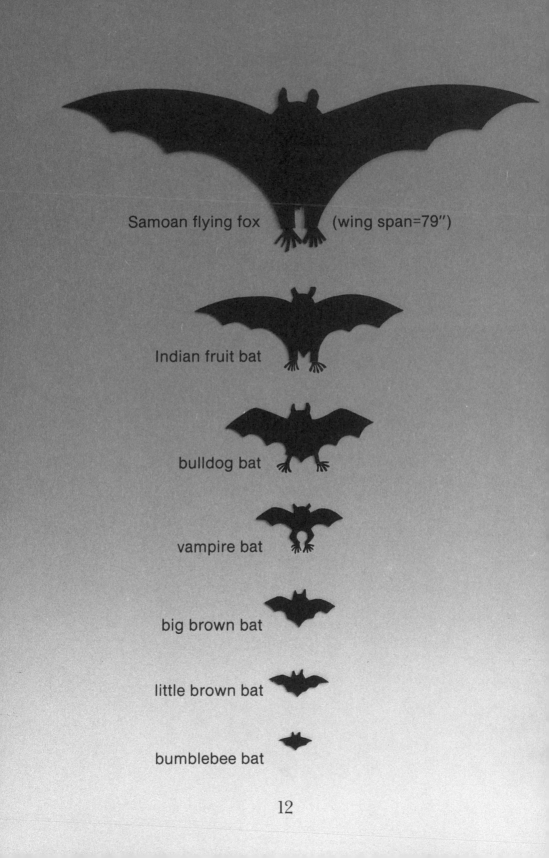

Samoan flying fox (wing span=79")

Indian fruit bat

bulldog bat

vampire bat

big brown bat

little brown bat

bumblebee bat

There are about 1,000

different kinds of bats

in the world.

The largest bat is called

the Samoan flying fox.

From wing to wing

it is as big as a Canada goose.

The smallest is the bumblebee bat.

You have probably heard

of the vampire bat.

Does the vampire bat

really drink the blood of animals?

Yes, it does.

It lives in Mexico and South America

where it bites cows and horses.

Are vampire bats dangerous to people?

No.

Like other bats, they are less dangerous

than raccoons, skunks, and

other wild creatures.

What do other bats like to eat?

Some eat fruit.

Some drink the juices of flowers,

just as hummingbirds do.

16

The bulldog bat even catches fish!

But most bats eat insects—

flies, moths, and mosquitoes.

This spotted bat

is about to catch a moth.

How can it find insects

in the dark?

It uses its ears!

A bat makes noises

when it flies—

click, click, click!

18

A moth flies by.

The clicks bounce off the moth.

They make an echo.

The echo tells the bat

where the moth is.

The bat moves very fast.

It scoops up the moth

with the tip of its wing.

Bats hunt only at night.

During the day they sleep.

This old barn is home to about

100 little brown bats.

The tired bats fly in
through a hole in the roof.
They grab the rafters
with their back feet.
All day long they will
hang upside down.
This is how bats sleep.

All the little brown bats

in the barn are females.

They like the barn.

It is warm and quiet.

Nobody uses it.

It will be a safe place

to bring up their young.

This little brown bat

is ready to have her baby.

She hangs by her front claws.

The baby comes out of her body.

The mother bat has a flap of skin

between her legs.

She spreads out the flap

and catches the baby in it.

The mother has to move fast!

It is a long way

to the floor of the barn.

Soon there are almost

100 baby bats in the old barn.

At night, the mother bats

go out to hunt.

When they come back,

all the babies are crying for food—

wheek, wheek, wheek!

Each mother knows her own baby's voice.

She flies right to it.

She washes its face

and lets it drink some of her milk.

By the end of August,

the nights are getting colder.

The mother cannot find enough

insects to eat.

It is time for the little brown bats

to move to a different home

for the winter.

Night after night they fly.

One morning, just before sunrise,

they come to a big cave.

Male and female bats

will sleep in the cave all winter.

Thousands of bats

come back to the same cave

every year.

When spring comes,

the bats wake up slowly.

They squeak and fly

around the cave.

Then one evening, all the bats

fly out the door of the cave.

Whoosh!

Outside the cave,

a barn owl

sits high in a tree.

Suddenly the owl swoops down!

Just in time, the young bat

darts out of the way.

The little brown bat

may live to be 20 years old.

During the summers

he will not live with his mother.

He will join a group of male bats

under an old bridge.

Little brown bats usually live

in the country.

Another kind of bat,

the big brown bat,

is often seen in cities.

Sometimes it sleeps

in church steeples

or in attics.

A big brown bat may even fly
right through an open window.

Big brown bats are

peaceful animals.

If one gets into your house,

don't be scared.

It is probably a young bat.

It is probably lost

and scared, too.

Why are so many people
afraid of bats?
Maybe they have heard that bats
like to land in people's hair.
But that's not true!

Some people even believe
stories about vampires—
like Count Dracula.
Dracula could turn into a bat.
He drank the blood
of sleeping people.
But Dracula is not a real person.
You will only meet him in books
and horror movies.

In China people are not afraid of bats.

They think that seeing a bat is good luck.

A good gift is a lucky charm

with a picture of five flying bats.

It is a sign of happiness.

Years ago there were many more bats.

Some caves had millions of them.

Now many of those caves

have been filled in.

Some have been turned into tunnels

for cars.

Hikers sometimes disturb bats, too.

If bats wake up

in the middle of winter,

they can starve to death.

This is because there are no

insects to eat!

Now scientists are starting

to protect bat caves.

Some people are even building

bat houses.

Bats can live in them

during the summer.

Bats help to control insects.

A tiny bat can catch

up to 600 mosquitoes in an hour.

One thing bats do <u>not</u> like is pollution.

If there are lots of bats around,

it means the air and water

are probably clean.

That's why it really is good luck

to see a bat!